Once Upon a Bowl of Oatmeal

70 Easy, Delicious, and Healthy Recipes
(Gluten-Free and Vegan)
to Transform those Boring Oats in the Back of Your Cupboard
into a Mouth-Watering Treat

by Annie Douglass Lima

Cover Art by Savannah Jezowski

Photography by Denise Johnson

Once Upon a Bowl of Oatmeal: 70 Easy, Delicious, and Healthy Recipes (Gluten Free and Vegan) to Transform those Boring Oats in the Back of Your Cupboard into a Mouth-Watering Treat

ISBN: 9781694184801

DELIGHTFUL OATMEALS EAGER TO MAKE YOUR ACQUAINTANCE:

INTRODUCTION

Today's busy families need a quick and healthy way to begin the day. If you're looking for breakfast options that won't leave you craving a donut an hour later, you've come to the right place. And while some might think it would take magic to make a bowl of oatmeal delicious, others believe it just takes the right recipe. In this book, I'm happy to present you with a little of both!

I've spent over two years experimenting and innovating to find tasty combinations of ingredients that will transform a bowl of oatmeal from basic porridge into a delicious and filling treat. As a busy teacher, I know the importance of quick breakfasts that provide lasting energy for a productive morning, and you'll find lots of them in these pages! Try out these recipes and discover new and delicious ways to start your day.

Why waste even one more morning with an unhealthy breakfast that won't satisfy you for long, or with no breakfast at all? Turn to the table of contents, choose a recipe that catches your eye, and plan to make that one tomorrow. It will give you a reason to get out of bed!

ABOUT THE RECIPES

You can use any kind of oats for these recipes: old-fashioned, quick-cooking, steel-cut, etc. Each kind has its own requirements in terms of cooking time (and the rules can change depending on whether you prefer the stovetop or microwave). So the first step in each of these recipes is usually to cook the oats with the liquid according to the instructions on your particular package of oats before adding the other ingredients.

Serving sizes indicated are for hungry adults. For light eaters or kids, consider reducing the quantities.

A Few Options:

- Reduce or skip the sugar to suit your taste, especially if your fruit is sweet.
- Substitute honey, stevia, molasses, or another sweetener for sugar.
- Add ⅛ teaspoon salt per serving to any recipe that doesn't already call for it.
- For extra fiber and protein, add a spoonful of chia seed, ground flax seed, and/or almond meal.
- For thicker oatmeal, reduce the amount of liquid by ¼ cup per serving.
- For richer oatmeal, substitute milk (dairy, coconut, almond, etc.) when a recipe calls for water.
- Add a mashed banana (one per serving) to any recipe that doesn't already call for it. It won't change the flavor (much), but it will make the oatmeal creamier and a little sweeter.

HERE WE GO 'ROUND THE MAPLE MULBERRY BUSH

Ingredients: No. of Servings:	oats	water	lemon juice	mul- berries	vanilla	maple syrup
1	½ cup	1 cup	¼ tsp.	½ cup	½ tsp.	2 Tbsp.
2	1 cup	2 cups	½ tsp.	1 cup	1 tsp.	¼ cup
3	1½ cups	3 cups	¾ tsp.	1½ cups	1½ tsp.	¼ cup + 2 Tbsp.
4	2 cups	4 cups	1 tsp.	2 cups	2 tsp.	½ cup
5	2½ cups	5 cups	1¼ tsp.	2½ cups	2½ tsp.	½ cup + 2 Tbsp.
6	3 cups	6 cups	1½ tsp.	3 cups	1 Tbsp.	¾ cup

Instructions: Cook the oats, water, and lemon juice according to oats package instructions. Mix in the other ingredients and heat, stirring, until everything is uniformly warm. Spoon into bowls and serve.

NUTCRACKER'S DREAM: MAPLE WALNUT

Ingredients: No. of Servings:	oats	water	walnuts	maple syrup
1	½ cup	1 cup	¼ cup	2 Tbsp.
2	1 cup	2 cups	½ cup	¼ cup
3	1½ cups	3 cups	¾ cup	¼ cup + 2 Tbsp.
4	2 cups	4 cups	1 cup	½ cup
5	2½ cups	5 cups	1¼ cups	½ cup + 2 Tbsp.
6	3 cups	6 cups	1½ cups	¾ cup

Instructions: Cook the oats and water according to oats package instructions. Mix in the other ingredients and heat, stirring, until everything is uniformly warm. Spoon into bowls and serve.

FRUITY MAPLE

Ingredients: / No. of Servings:	oats	water	any kind of fruit, chopped or mashed	apple-sauce	raisins	maple syrup
1	½ cup	¾ cup	¼ cup	¼ cup	¼ cup	2 Tbsp.
2	1 cup	1½ cups	½ cup	½ cup	½ cup	¼ cup
3	1½ cups	2¼ cups	¾ cup	¾ cup	¾ cup	¼ cup + 2 Tbsp.
4	2 cups	3 cups	1 cup	1 cup	1 cup	½ cup
5	2½ cups	3¾ cups	1¼ cups	1¼ cups	1¼ cups	½ cup + 2 Tbsp.
6	3 cups	4½ cups	1½ cups	1½ cups	1½ cups	¾ cup

Instructions: Cook the oats and water according to oats package instructions. Mix in the other ingredients and heat, stirring, until everything is uniformly warm. (I recommend using unsweetened applesauce. If yours is sweetened, you may want to decrease the maple syrup.) Spoon into bowls and serve.

OGRE'S ORANGE PECAN

Ingredients: / No. of Servings:	oats	water	orange juice	pecans, chopped	cinna-mon	ginger	cloves	maple syrup
1	½ cup	⅓ cup	⅔ cup	¼ cup	½ tsp.	¼ tsp.	⅛ tsp.	1 Tbsp.
2	1 cup	⅔ cup	1⅓ cups	½ cup	1 tsp.	½ tsp.	¼ tsp.	2 Tbsp.
3	1½ cups	1 cups	2 cups	¾ cup	1½ tsp.	¾ tsp.	⅜ tsp.	3 Tbsp.
4	2 cups	1⅓ cups	2⅔ cups	1 cup	2 tsp.	1 tsp.	½ tsp.	¼ cup
5	2½ cups	1⅔ cups	3⅓ cups	1¼ cups	2½ tsp.	1¼ tsp.	⅝ tsp.	¼ cup + 1 Tbsp.
6	3 cups	2 cups	4 cups	1½ cups	1 Tbsp.	1½ tsp.	¾ tsp.	¼ cup + 2 Tbsp.

Instructions: Cook the oats with the water and orange juice according to oats package instructions. Mix in the other ingredients and heat, stirring, until everything is uniformly warm. Spoon into bowls and serve.

ALADDIN'S BAKLAVA

Ingredients: / No. of Servings:	oats	water	lemon juice	cinnamon	pistachios	honey
1	½ cup	1 cup	½ tsp.	¾ tsp.	½ cup	2 Tbsp.
2	1 cup	2 cups	1 tsp.	1½ tsp.	1 cup	¼ cup
3	1½ cups	3 cups	1½ tsp.	2¼ tsp.	1½ cups	¼ cup + 2 Tbsp.
4	2 cups	4 cups	2 tsp.	1 Tbsp.	2 cups	½ cup
5	2½ cups	5 cups	2½ tsp.	1 Tbsp. + ¾ tsp.	2½ cups	½ cup + 2 Tbsp.
6	3 cups	6 cups	1 Tbsp.	1 Tbsp. + 1½ tsp.	3 cups	¾ cup

Instructions: Cook the oats with the water and lemon juice according to oats package instructions. Mix in the other ingredients and heat, stirring, until everything is uniformly warm. (For a vegan option, use Bee Free Honee or another honey substitute.) Spoon into bowls and serve.

CRUNCHY CRANBERRY WALNUT

Ingredients: No. of Servings:	oats	water	dried cranberries	walnuts, chopped	brown sugar
1	½ cup	1 cup	⅓ cup	⅓ cup	2 Tbsp.
2	1 cup	2 cups	⅔ cup	⅔ cup	¼ cup
3	1½ cups	3 cups	1 cup	1 cup	¼ cup + 2 Tbsp.
4	2 cups	4 cups	1⅓ cups	1⅓ cups	½ cup
5	2½ cups	5 cups	1⅔ cups	1⅔ cups	½ cup + 2 Tbsp.
6	3 cups	6 cups	2 cups	2 cups	¾ cup

Instructions: Cook the oats and water according to oats package instructions. Mix in the other ingredients and heat, stirring, until everything is uniformly warm. Spoon into bowls and serve.

CRUNCHY
CRANBERRY WALNUT
OATMEAL

CHOCOLATE COCONUT

Ingredients: No. of Servings:	oats	water	coconut milk	grated coconut	chocolate syrup
1	½ cup	½ cup	½ cup	3 Tbsp.	2 Tbsp.
2	1 cup	1 cup	1 cup	¼ cup + 2 Tbsp.	¼ cup
3	1½ cups	1½ cups	1½ cups	½ cup + 1 Tbsp.	¼ cup + 2 Tbsp.
4	2 cups	2 cups	2 cups	¾ cup	½ cup
5	2½ cups	2½ cups	2½ cups	¾ cup + 3 Tbsp.	½ cup + 2 Tbsp.
6	3 cups	3 cups	3 cups	1 cup + 2 Tbsp.	¾ cup

Instructions: Cook the oats, water, and coconut milk according to oats package instructions. Mix in the other ingredients and heat, stirring, until everything is uniformly warm. Spoon into bowls and serve.

HANSEL'S GINGERBREAD CREAM CHEESE

Ingredients: / No. of Servings:	oats	water	cream cheese	ginger	cinna-mon	ground cloves	molasses
1	½ cup	1 cup	2 Tbsp.	¼ tsp.	½ tsp.	1 dash	2 Tbsp.
2	1 cup	2 cups	¼ cup	½ tsp.	1 tsp.	2 dashes	¼ cup
3	1½ cups	3 cups	¼ cup + 2 Tbsp.	¾ tsp.	1½ tsp.	3 dashes	¼ cup + 2 Tbsp.
4	2 cups	4 cups	½ cup	1 tsp.	2 tsp.	4 dashes	½ cup
5	2½ cups	5 cups	½ cup + 2 Tbsp.	1¼ tsp.	2½ tsp.	5 dashes	½ cup + 2 Tbsp.
6	3 cups	6 cups	¾ cup	1½ tsp.	1 Tbsp.	6 dashes	¾ cup

Instructions: Cook the oats and water according to oats package instructions. Mix in the other ingredients (for a vegan option, use your favorite plant-based cream cheese) and heat, stirring, until everything is uniformly warm. Spoon into bowls and serve. (Don't overdo it with the cloves – less is more!)

GRETEL'S GINGERBREAD PERSIMMON

Ingredients: / No. of Servings:	oats	water	persimmons, finely chopped or mashed	ginger	cinna-mon	ground cloves	molasses
1	½ cup	1 cup	1	¼ tsp.	¼ tsp.	1 small sprinkle	1 Tbsp. + 1 tsp.
2	1 cup	2 cups	2	½ tsp.	½ tsp.	2 small sprinkles	2 Tbsp. + 2 tsp.
3	1½ cups	3 cups	3	¾ tsp.	¾ tsp.	3 small sprinkles	4 Tbsp.
4	2 cups	4 cups	4	1 tsp.	1 tsp.	4 small sprinkles	5 Tbsp. + 1 tsp.
5	2½ cups	5 cups	5	1¼ tsp.	1¼ tsp.	5 small sprinkles	6 Tbsp. + 2 tsp.
6	3 cups	6 cups	6	1½ tsp.	1½ tsp.	6 small sprinkles	8 Tbsp.

Instructions: Cook the oats with the water according to oats package instructions. Mix in the other ingredients (be careful not to overdo it on the cloves – a little goes a long way!). Heat, stirring, until everything is uniformly warm. Spoon into bowls and serve.

THE WITCH'S GINGERBREAD WHITE CHOCOLATE

Ingredients: No. of Servings:	oats	water	molasses	ginger	cinna-mon	ground cloves	white chocolate chips
1	½ cup	1 cup	1½ Tbsp.	¼ tsp.	½ tsp.	⅛ tsp.	¼ cup
2	1 cup	2 cups	3 Tbsp.	½ tsp.	1 tsp.	¼ tsp.	½ cup
3	1½ cups	3 cups	4½ Tbsp.	¾ tsp.	1½ tsp.	⅜ tsp.	¾ cup
4	2 cups	4 cups	¼ cup + 2 Tbsp.	1 tsp.	2 tsp.	½ tsp.	1 cup
5	2½ cups	5 cups	¼ cup + 3 ½ Tbsp.	1¼ tsp.	2½ tsp.	⅝ tsp.	1¼ cups
6	3 cups	6 cups	½ cup + 1 Tbsp.	1½ tsp.	1 Tbsp.	¾ tsp.	1½ cups

Instructions: Cook the oats and water according to oats package instructions. Mix in the other ingredients and heat, stirring, until white chocolate has melted and everything is uniformly warm. Spoon into bowls and serve. (Or, don't add the white chocolate chips until the end. Sprinkle ¼ cup on each portion.)

AFTER THE BALL: CINDERELLA'S PUMPKIN SPICE

Ingredients: / No. of Servings:	oats	water	pumpkin puree	vanilla	pumpkin pie spice	salt	pecans, chopped	brown sugar
1	½ cup	1 cup	¼ cup	¼ tsp.	½ tsp.	¼ tsp.	¼ cup	2 Tbsp.
2	1 cup	2 cups	½ cup	½ tsp.	1 tsp.	½ tsp.	½ cup	¼ cup
3	1½ cups	3 cups	¾ cup	¾ tsp.	1 ½ tsp.	¾ tsp.	¾ cup	¼ cup + 2 Tbsp.
4	2 cups	4 cups	1 cup	1 tsp.	2 tsp.	1 tsp.	1 cup	½ cup
5	2½ cups	5 cups	1¼ cups	1¼ tsp.	2½ tsp.	1¼ tsp.	1¼ cups	½ cup + 2 Tbsp.
6	3 cups	6 cups	1½ cups	1½ tsp.	1 Tbsp.	1½ tsp.	1½ cups	¾ cup

Instructions: Cook the oats with the water according to oats package instructions. Mix in the other ingredients, except pecans. Heat, stirring, until everything is uniformly warm. Spoon into bowls and sprinkle ¼ cup chopped pecans over each portion before serving.

IF THE SHOE FITS: PRINCE CHARMING'S PUMPKIN SPICE LATTE

Ingredients: / No. of Servings:	oats	milk	pumpkin puree	instant coffee granules	pumpkin pie spice	white chocolate chips
1	½ cup	1 cup	½ cup	1 ½ tsp.	½ tsp.	⅓ cup
2	1 cup	2 cups	1 cup	1 Tbsp.	1 tsp.	⅔ cup
3	1½ cups	3 cups	1½ cups	1 Tbsp. + 1½ tsp.	1½ tsp.	1 cup
4	2 cups	4 cups	2 cups	2 Tbsp.	2 tsp.	1⅓ cups
5	2½ cups	5 cups	2½ cups	2 Tbsp. + 1½ tsp.	2½ tsp.	1⅔ cups
6	3 cups	6 cups	3 cups	3 Tbsp.	1 Tbsp.	2 cups

Instructions: Cook the oats with the milk and coffee according to oats package instructions. Mix in the other ingredients and heat, stirring, until the white chocolate chips have melted and everything is uniformly warm. Spoon into bowls and serve.

UNICORN'S DELIGHT: COCONUT VANILLA

Ingredients: No. of Servings:	oats	water	coconut milk	grated coconut	vanilla	brown sugar
1	½ cup	½ cup	½ cup	2 Tbsp.	¼ tsp.	2 Tbsp.
2	1 cup	1 cups	1 cups	¼ cup	½ tsp.	¼ cup
3	1½ cups	1½ cups	1½ cups	¼ cup + 2 Tbsp.	¾ tsp.	¼ cup + 2 Tbsp.
4	2 cups	2 cups	2 cups	½ cup	1 tsp.	½ cup
5	2½ cups	2½ cups	2½ cups	½ cup + 2 Tbsp.	1¼ tsp.	½ cup + 2 Tbsp.
6	3 cups	3 cups	3 cups	¾ cup	1½ tsp.	¾ cup

Instructions: Cook the oats, water, and coconut milk according to oats package instructions. Mix in the other ingredients and heat, stirring, until everything is uniformly warm. Spoon into bowls and serve. If desired, sprinkle additional grated or shredded coconut over each serving.

UNICORN'S DELIGHT
OATMEAL

THE SNOW QUEEN'S REVENGE: RASPBERRY VANILLA

Ingredients: No. of Servings:	oats	water	rasp-berries	vanilla	brown sugar
1	½ cup	1 cup	½ cup	½ tsp.	2 Tbsp.
2	1 cup	2 cups	1 cup	1 tsp.	¼ cup
3	1½ cups	3 cups	1½ cups	1½ tsp.	¼ cup + 2 Tbsp.
4	2 cups	4 cups	2 cups	2 tsp.	½ cup
5	2½ cups	5 cups	2½ cups	2½ tsp.	½ cup + 2 Tbsp.
6	3 cups	6 cups	3 cups	1 Tbsp.	¾ cup

Instructions: Cook the oats and water according to oats package instructions. Mix in the other ingredients and heat, stirring, until everything is uniformly warm. Spoon into bowls and serve.

MARY, MARY'S ALMOND BERRY

Ingredients: No. of Servings:	oats	water	coconut milk or almond milk	your favorite berries	grated coconut	brown sugar
1	⅓ cup	½ cup	½ cup	½ cup	¼ cup	2 Tbsp.
2	⅔ cup	1 cup	1 cup	1 cup	½ cup	¼ cup
3	1 cup	1½ cups	1½ cups	1½ cups	¾ cup	¼ cup + 2 Tbsp.
4	1⅓ cups	2 cups	2 cups	2 cups	1 cup	½ cup
5	1⅔ cups	2½ cups	2½ cups	2½ cups	1¼ cups	½ cup + 2 Tbsp.
6	2 cups	3 cups	3 cups	3 cups	1½ cups	¾ cup

Instructions: Cook the oats, water, and coconut/almond milk according to oats package instructions. (This is extra tasty if you use a combination of coconut and almond milks.) Mix in the other ingredients (for the berries, feel free to combine multiple kinds). Heat, stirring, until everything is uniformly warm. Spoon into bowls and serve. Optional: add a sprinkling of slivered almonds to each portion before serving.

CINNAMON ALMOND

Ingredients: No. of Servings:	oats	water	cinnamon	almonds, slivered	almond meal or almond flour	brown sugar
1	½ cup	1 cup	¾ tsp.	2 Tbsp.	2 Tbsp.	2 Tbsp.
2	1 cup	2 cups	1½ tsp.	¼ cup	¼ cup	¼ cup
3	1½ cups	3 cups	2¼ tsp.	¼ cup + 2 Tbsp.	¼ cup + 2 Tbsp.	¼ cup + 2 Tbsp.
4	2 cups	4 cups	1 Tbsp.	½ cup	½ cup	½ cup
5	2½ cups	5 cups	1 Tbsp. + ¾ tsp.	½ cup + 2 Tbsp.	½ cup + 2 Tbsp.	½ cup + 2 Tbsp.
6	3 cups	6 cups	1 Tbsp. + 1½ tsp.	¾ cup	¾ cup	¾ cup

Instructions: Cook the oats and water according to oats package instructions. Mix in the other ingredients and heat, stirring, until everything is uniformly warm. Spoon into bowls and serve.

GOLDILOCKS' "JUST RIGHT" ALMOND JOY

Ingredients: No. of Servings:	oats	water and coconut milk	grated coconut	chocolate syrup	almond meal/ almond flour
1	½ cup	½ cup each	2 Tbsp.	2 Tbsp.	3 Tbsp.
2	1 cup	1 cup each	¼ cup	¼ cup	¼ cup + 2 Tbsp.
3	1½ cups	1½ cups each	¼ cup + 2 Tbsp.	¼ cup + 2 Tbsp.	½ cup + 1 Tbsp.
4	2 cups	2 cups each	½ cup	½ cup	¾ cup
5	2½ cups	2½ cups each	½ cup + 2 Tbsp.	½ cup + 2 Tbsp.	¾ cup + 3 Tbsp.
6	3 cups	3 cups each	¾ cup	¾ cup	1 cup + 2 Tbsp.

Instructions: Cook the oats, water, and coconut milk according to oats package instructions. Mix in the other ingredients and heat, stirring, until everything is uniformly warm. Spoon into bowls and serve. (If you like, sprinkle slivered almonds over each portion before serving.)

BRIAR ROSE'S STRAWBERRY KIWI

Ingredients: No. of Servings:	oats	water	strawberries, chopped or mashed	kiwis, chopped or mashed	brown sugar
1	½ cup	1 cup	¼ cup	1	2 Tbsp.
2	1 cup	2 cups	½ cup	2	¼ cup
3	1½ cups	3 cups	¾ cup	3	¼ cup + 2 Tbsp.
4	2 cups	4 cups	1 cup	4	½ cup
5	2½ cups	5 cups	1¼ cups	5	½ cup + 2 Tbsp.
6	3 cups	6 cups	1½ cups	6	¾ cup

Instructions: Cook the oats and water according to oats package instructions. Mix in the other ingredients and heat, stirring, until everything is uniformly warm. Spoon into bowls and serve.

BRIAR ROSE'S
STRAWBERRY KIWI OATMEAL

THE FROG PRINCE'S LEMON KIWI

Ingredients: / No. of Servings:	oats	water and coconut milk	lemon juice	kiwis, finely chopped or mashed	grated coconut	brown sugar
1	½ cup	½ cup each	2 tsp.	1	3 Tbsp.	3 Tbsp.
2	1 cup	1 cup each	1 Tbsp. + 1 tsp.	2	¼ cup + 2 Tbsp.	¼ cup + 2 Tbsp.
3	1½ cups	1½ cups each	2 Tbsp.	3	½ cup + 1 Tbsp.	½ cup + 1 Tbsp.
4	2 cups	2 cups each	2 Tbsp. + 2 tsp.	4	¾ cup	¾ cup
5	2½ cups	2½ cups each	3 Tbsp. + 1 tsp.	5	¾ cup + 3 Tbsp.	¾ cup + 3 Tbsp.
6	3 cups	3 cups each	4 Tbsp.	6	1 cup + 2 Tbsp.	1 cup + 2 Tbsp.

Instructions: Cook the oats, water, coconut milk, and lemon juice according to oats package instructions. Mix in the other ingredients and heat, stirring, until everything is uniformly warm. Spoon into bowls and serve.

DANCE OF THE LEMON PLUM FAIRY

Ingredients: / No. of Servings:	oats	water	lemon juice	large plums, chopped	ground ginger	salt	maple syrup
1	½ cup	1 cup	¼ tsp.	1	¼ tsp.	⅛ tsp.	2 Tbsp.
2	1 cup	2 cups	½ tsp.	2	½ tsp.	¼ tsp.	¼ cup
3	1½ cups	3 cups	¾ tsp.	3	¾ tsp.	⅜ tsp.	¼ cup + 2 Tbsp.
4	2 cups	4 cups	1 tsp.	4	1 tsp.	½ tsp.	½ cup
5	2½ cups	5 cups	1¼ tsp.	5	1¼ tsp.	⅝ tsp.	½ cup + 2 Tbsp.
6	3 cups	6 cups	1½ tsp.	6	1½ tsp.	¾ tsp.	¾ cup

Instructions: Cook the oats with the water and lemon juice according to oats package instructions. Mix in the other ingredients and heat, stirring, until everything is uniformly warm. Spoon into bowls and serve.

EAST OF THE SUN AND WEST OF THE MOON: COCONUT LEMON

Ingredients: / No. of Servings:	oats	water	coconut milk	lemon juice	grated coconut	brown sugar
1	½ cup	½ cup	½ cup	1 Tbsp.	¼ cup	2 Tbsp.
2	1 cup	1 cup	1 cup	2 Tbsp.	½ cup	¼ cup
3	1½ cups	1½ cups	1½ cups	3 Tbsp.	¾ cup	¼ cup + 2 Tbsp.
4	2 cups	2 cups	2 cups	¼ cup	1 cup	½ cup
5	2½ cups	2½ cups	2½ cups	¼ cup + 1 Tbsp.	1¼ cups	½ cup + 2 Tbsp.
6	3 cups	3 cups	3 cups	¼ cup + 2 Tbsp.	1½ cups	¾ cup

Instructions: Cook the oats, water, coconut milk, and lemon juice according to oats package instructions. Mix in the other ingredients and heat, stirring, until everything is uniformly warm. Spoon into bowls and serve.

SLEEPING BEAUTY'S WAKE-UP CALL: MOCHA

Ingredients: No. of Servings:	oats	strong brewed coffee (with milk/creamer if you prefer)	bananas, mashed	chocolate syrup
1	½ cup	1 cup	1	2 Tbsp.
2	1 cup	2 cups	2	¼ cup
3	1½ cups	3 cups	3	¼ cup + 2 Tbsp.
4	2 cups	4 cups	4	½ cup
5	2 ½ cups	5 cups	5	½ cup + 2 Tbsp.
6	3 cups	6 cups	6	¾ cup

Instructions: Cook the oats and coffee according to oats package instructions. Mix in the other ingredients and heat, stirring, until everything is uniformly warm. Spoon into bowls and serve.

TROPICAL WAKE-UP CALL: COCONUT MOCHA

Ingredients: / No. of Servings:	oats	strong brewed coffee	coconut milk	grated coconut	chocolate syrup	vanilla
1	½ cup	⅔ cup	⅓ cup	3 Tbsp.	2 Tbsp.	½ tsp.
2	1 cup	1⅓ cups	⅔ cup	¼ cup + 2 Tbsp.	¼ cup	1 tsp.
3	1½ cups	2 cups	1 cup	½ cup + 1 Tbsp.	¼ cup + 2 Tbsp.	1½ tsp.
4	2 cups	2⅔ cups	1⅓ cups	¾ cup	½ cup	2 tsp.
5	2½ cups	3⅓ cups	1⅔ cups	¾ cup + 3 Tbsp.	½ cup + 2 Tbsp.	2½ tsp.
6	3 cups	4 cups	2 cups	1 cup + 2 Tbsp.	¾ cup	1 Tbsp.

Instructions: Cook the oats with the coffee and coconut milk according to oats package instructions. Mix in the other ingredients and heat, stirring, until everything is uniformly warm. Spoon into bowls and serve.

CONSIDER THE COCONUT CASHEW

Ingredients: / No. of Servings:	oats	water	coconut milk	cashews, toasted	grated coconut	brown sugar
1	½ cup	½ cup	½ cup	⅓ cup	2 Tbsp.	2 Tbsp.
2	1 cup	1 cup	1 cup	⅔ cup	¼ cup	¼ cup
3	1½ cups	1½ cups	1½ cups	1 cup	¼ cup + 2 Tbsp.	¼ cup + 2 Tbsp.
4	2 cups	2 cups	2 cups	1⅓ cups	½ cup	½ cup
5	2½ cups	2½ cups	2½ cups	1⅔ cups	½ cup + 2 Tbsp.	½ cup + 2 Tbsp.
6	3 cups	3 cups	3 cups	2 cups	¾ cup	¾ cup

Instructions: Cook the oats, water, and coconut milk according to oats package instructions. Mix in the other ingredients and heat, stirring, until everything is uniformly warm. Spoon into bowls and serve.

COCONUT ALMOND

Ingredients: No. of Servings:	oats	water and coconut milk	almond meal or almond flour	almonds, slivered	grated coconut	brown sugar
1	½ cup	½ cup each	2 Tbsp.	2 Tbsp.	2 Tbsp.	2 Tbsp.
2	1 cup	1 cup each	¼ cup	¼ cup	¼ cup	¼ cup
3	1½ cups	1½ cups each	¼ cup + 2 Tbsp.	¼ cup + 2 Tbsp.	¼ cup + 2 Tbsp.	¼ cup + 2 Tbsp.
4	2 cups	2 cups each	½ cup	½ cup	½ cup	½ cup
5	2½ cups	2½ cups each	½ cup + 2 Tbsp.	½ cup + 2 Tbsp.	½ cup + 2 Tbsp.	½ cup + 2 Tbsp.
6	3 cups	3 cups each	¾ cup	¾ cup	¾ cup	¾ cup

Instructions: Cook the oats, water, and coconut milk according to oats package instructions. Mix in the other ingredients and heat, stirring, until everything is uniformly warm. Spoon into bowls and serve.

COCONUT ALMOND
OATMEAL

COCONUT KIWI

Ingredients: No. of Servings:	oats	water	coconut milk	kiwis, finely chopped or mashed	grated coconut	brown sugar
1	½ cup	½ cup	½ cup	1	¼ cup	2 Tbsp.
2	1 cup	1 cups	1 cups	2	½ cup	¼ cup
3	1½ cups	1½ cups	1½ cups	3	¾ cup	⅓ cup + 1 Tbsp.
4	2 cups	2 cups	2 cups	4	1 cup	½ cup
5	2½ cups	2½ cups	2½ cups	5	1¼ cups	½ cup + 2 Tbsp.
6	3 cups	3 cups	3 cups	6	1½ cups	¾ cup

Instructions: Cook the oats, water, and coconut milk according to oats package instructions. Mix in the other ingredients and heat, stirring, until everything is uniformly warm. Spoon into bowls and serve.

CHOCOLATE COCONUT KIWI

Ingredients: / No. of Servings:	oats	water	coconut milk and grated coconut	kiwis, finely chopped or mashed	cocoa powder	brown sugar
1	½ cup	⅔ cups	⅓ cup each	1	1 Tbsp.	2 Tbsp.
2	1 cup	1⅓ cups	⅔ cup each	2	2 Tbsp.	¼ cup
3	1½ cups	2 cups	1 cup each	3	3 Tbsp.	¼ cup + 2 Tbsp.
4	2 cups	2⅔ cups	1⅓ cups each	4	¼ cup	½ cup
5	2½ cups	3⅓ cups	1⅔ cups each	5	¼ cup + 1 Tbsp.	½ cup + 2 Tbsp.
6	3 cups	4 cups	2 cups each	6	¼ cup + 2 Tbsp.	¾ cup

Instructions: Cook the oats, water, and coconut milk according to oats package instructions. Mix in the other ingredients and heat, stirring, until everything is uniformly warm. Spoon into bowls and serve.

SWEET POTATO COCONUT

Ingredients: / No. of Servings:	oats	water	coconut milk	cooked sweet potato, mashed	grated coconut	maple syrup
1	½ cup	½ cup	½ cup	⅓ cup	2 Tbsp.	1½ Tbsp.
2	1 cup	1 cup	1 cup	⅔ cup	¼ cup	3 Tbsp.
3	1½ cups	1½ cups	1½ cups	1 cup	¼ cup + 2 Tbsp.	¼ cup + ½ Tbsp.
4	2 cups	2 cups	2 cups	1⅓ cups	½ cup	¼ cup + 2 Tbsp.
5	2½ cups	2½ cups	2½ cups	1⅔ cups	½ cup + 2 Tbsp.	¼ cup + 3½ Tbsp.
6	3 cups	3 cups	3 cups	2 cups	¾ cup	½ cup + 1 Tbsp.

Instructions: Cook the oats, water, and coconut milk according to oats package instructions. Mix in the other ingredients and heat, stirring, until everything is uniformly warm. Spoon into bowls and serve.

MANGO COCONUT

Ingredients: No. of Servings:	oats	mango juice, syrup from canned mangoes, or coconut milk	mango, chopped	grated coconut	brown sugar
1	½ cup	1 cup	½ cup	2 Tbsp.	2 Tbsp.
2	1 cup	2 cups	1 cup	¼ cup	¼ cup
3	1½ cups	3 cups	1½ cups	¼ cup + 2 Tbsp.	¼ cup + 2 Tbsp.
4	2 cups	4 cups	2 cups	½ cup	½ cup
5	2½ cups	5 cups	2½ cups	½ cup + 2 Tbsp.	½ cup + 2 Tbsp.
6	3 cups	6 cups	3 cups	¾ cup	¾ cup

Instructions: Cook the oats and juice/syrup/coconut milk (feel free to use a combination) according to oats package instructions. Mix in the other ingredients and heat, stirring, until everything is uniformly warm. (Reduce or skip the sugar if using mango syrup or sweetened juice.) Spoon into bowls and serve.

CREAMY MANGO COCONUT SPICE

Ingredients: No. of Servings:	oats and mango, chopped or mashed	water	coco-nut milk	grated coco-nut	cinna-mon	ground car-damom	ground cloves and nutmeg	mo-lasses	small bananas, mashed
1	½ cup each	⅔ cups	⅓ cup	¼ cup	¾ tsp.	½ tsp.	⅛ tsp. each	2 Tbsp.	1
2	1 cup each	1⅓ cups	⅔ cup	½ cup	1½ tsp.	1 tsp.	¼ tsp. each	¼ cup	2
3	1½ cups each	2 cups	1 cup	¾ cup	2¼ tsp.	1½ tsp.	⅜ tsp. each	¼ cup + 2 Tbsp.	3
4	2 cups each	2⅔ cups	1⅓ cups	1 cup	1 Tbsp.	2 tsp.	½ tsp. each	½ cup	4
5	2½ cups each	3⅓ cups	1 ⅔ cups	1¼ cups	1 Tbsp. + ¾ tsp.	2½ tsp.	⅝ tsp. each	½ cup + 2 Tbsp.	5
6	3 cups each	4 cups	2 cups	1½ cups	1 Tbsp. + 1½ tsp.	1 Tbsp.	¾ tsp. each	¾ cup	6

Instructions: Cook the oats, water, and coconut milk according to oats package instructions. Mix in the other ingredients and heat, stirring, until everything is uniformly warm. Spoon into bowls and serve.

CREAMY
MANGO COCONUT SPICE
OATMEAL

MANGO BANANA

Ingredients: / No. of Servings:	oats	water	mango juice/ syrup from canned mangoes/ coconut milk	mango, finely chopped or mashed	ground car-damom	brown sugar	small bananas, mashed
1	¼ cup	½ cup	¼ cup	½ cup	½ tsp.	2 Tbsp.	1
2	½ cup	1 cup	½ cup	1 cup	1 tsp.	¼ cup	2
3	¾ cup	1½ cups	¾ cup	1½ cups	1½ tsp.	¼ cup + 2 Tbsp.	3
4	1 cup	2 cups	1 cup	2 cups	2 tsp.	½ cup	4
5	1¼ cups	2½ cups	1¼ cups	2½ cups	2½ tsp.	½ cup + 2 Tbsp.	5
6	1½ cups	3 cups	1½ cups	3 cups	1 Tbsp.	¾ cup	6

Instructions: Cook the oats and juice/syrup/coconut milk (feel free to use a combination) according to oats package instructions. Mix in the other ingredients and heat, stirring, until everything is uniformly warm. (Reduce or skip the sugar if using syrup or sweetened juice.) Spoon into bowls and serve.

THE GINGERBREAD MAN'S GINGERY MANGO PINEAPPLE

Ingredients: / No. of Servings:	oats	water	mango (chopped or mashed)	pineapple (chopped or mashed)	ground ginger	brown sugar
1	½ cup	1 cup	½ cup	¼ cup	¼ tsp.	2 Tbsp.
2	1 cup	2 cups	1 cup	½ cup	½ tsp.	¼ cup
3	1½ cups	3 cups	1½ cups	¾ cup	¾ tsp.	¼ cup + 2 Tbsp.
4	2 cups	4 cups	2 cups	1 cup	1 tsp.	½ cup
5	2½ cups	5 cups	2½ cups	1¼ cups	1¼ tsp.	½ cup + 2 Tbsp.
6	3 cups	6 cups	3 cups	1½ cups	1½ tsp.	¾ cup

Instructions: Cook the oats and water according to oats package instructions. Mix in the other ingredients and heat, stirring, until everything is uniformly warm. Spoon into bowls and serve.

STRAWBERRY PINEAPPLE

Ingredients: / No. of Servings:	oats	water	pineapple, chopped or pureed	strawberries, chopped or pureed	brown sugar
1	½ cup	1 cup	½ cup	¼ cup	2 Tbsp.
2	1 cup	2 cups	1 cup	½ cup	¼ cup
3	1½ cups	3 cups	1½ cups	¾ cup	¼ cup + 2 Tbsp.
4	2 cups	4 cups	2 cups	1 cup	½ cup
5	2½ cups	5 cups	2½ cups	1¼ cups	½ cup + 2 Tbsp.
6	3 cups	6 cups	3 cups	1½ cups	¾ cup

Instructions: Cook the oats and water according to oats package instructions. (If pureeing the fruit, leave out half the water and cook the liquid fruity mixture with the oats and the rest of the water.) Mix in the other ingredients. Heat, stirring, until everything is uniformly warm. Spoon into bowls and serve.

STRAWBERRY COCONUT

Ingredients: / No. of Servings:	oats	water	coconut milk	strawberries, chopped	grated coconut	brown sugar
1	½ cup	½ cup	½ cup	½ cup	3 Tbsp.	2 Tbsp.
2	1 cup	1 cup	1 cup	1 cup	¼ cup + 2 Tbsp.	¼ cup
3	1½ cups	1½ cups	1½ cups	1½ cups	½ cup + 1 Tbsp.	¼ cup + 2 Tbsp.
4	2 cups	2 cups	2 cups	2 cups	¾ cup	½ cup
5	2½ cups	2½ cups	2½ cups	2½ cups	¾ cup + 3 Tbsp.	½ cup + 2 Tbsp.
6	3 cups	3 cups	3 cups	3 cups	1 cup + 2 Tbsp.	¾ cup

Instructions: Cook the oats, water, and coconut milk according to oats package instructions. Mix in the other ingredients and heat, stirring, until everything is uniformly warm. Spoon into bowls and serve.

RED RIDING HOOD'S TANGY STRAWBERRY CRUNCH

Ingredients: No. of Servings:	oats	water	milk	lemon juice	straw-berries	walnuts, chopped	brown sugar
1	½ cup	¼ cup	¾ cup	1 Tbsp.	½ cup	¼ cup	2 Tbsp.
2	1 cup	½ cup	1½ cups	2 Tbsp.	1 cup	½ cup	¼ cup
3	1½ cups	¾ cup	2¼ cups	3 Tbsp.	1½ cups	¾ cup	¼ cup + 2 Tbsp.
4	2 cups	1 cup	3 cups	¼ cup	2 cups	1 cup	½ cup
5	2½ cups	1¼ cups	3¾ cups	¼ cup + 1 Tbsp.	2½ cups	1¼ cups	½ cup + 2 Tbsp.
6	3 cups	1½ cups	4½ cups	¼ cup + 2 Tbsp.	3 cups	1½ cups	¾ cup

Instructions: Puree the strawberries in a blender with the water. Combine with milk (for a vegan option, use your favorite plant-based milk), lemon juice, and oats and cook according to oats package instructions. Mix in the other ingredients and heat, stirring, until everything is uniformly warm. Spoon into bowls and serve.

STRAWBERRY BANANA

Ingredients: / No. of Servings:	oats	water	bananas, mashed	straw-berries, chopped or mashed	brown sugar
1	½ cup	1 cup	1	½ cup	2 Tbsp.
2	1 cup	2 cups	2	1 cup	¼ cup
3	1½ cups	3 cups	3	1½ cups	¼ cup + 2 Tbsp.
4	2 cups	4 cups	4	2 cups	½ cup
5	2½ cups	5 cups	5	2½ cups	½ cup + 2 Tbsp.
6	3 cups	6 cups	6	3 cups	¾ cup

Instructions: Cook the oats and water according to oats package instructions. Mix in the other ingredients and heat, stirring, until everything is uniformly warm. Spoon into bowls and serve.

STRAWBERRY ALMOND

Ingredients: No. of Servings:	oats	almond milk	almond meal or almond flour	straw-berries, chopped or mashed	almonds, slivered	brown sugar
1	½ cup	1 cup	2 Tbsp.	½ cup	¼ cup	2 Tbsp.
2	1 cup	2 cups	¼ cup	1 cup	½ cup	¼ cup
3	1½ cups	3 cups	¼ cup + 2 Tbsp.	1½ cups	¾ cup	¼ cup + 2 Tbsp.
4	2 cups	4 cups	½ cup	2 cups	1 cup	½ cup
5	2½ cups	5 cups	½ cup + 2 Tbsp.	2½ cups	1¼ cups	½ cup + 2 Tbsp.
6	3 cups	6 cups	¾ cup	3 cups	1½ cups	¾ cup

Instructions: Cook the oats and almond milk according to oats package instructions. Mix in the other ingredients and heat, stirring, until everything is uniformly warm. Spoon into bowls and serve.

STRAWBERRY ALMOND
OATMEAL

STRAWBERRY MULBERRY

Ingredients: / No. of Servings:	oats	water	straw-berries, mashed	mul-berries, mashed	cinnamon	brown sugar
1	½ cup	1 cup	⅓ cup	⅓ cup	¼ tsp.	2 Tbsp.
2	1 cup	2 cups	⅔ cup	⅔ cup	½ tsp.	¼ cup
3	1½ cups	3 cups	1 cup	1 cup	¾ tsp.	¼ cup + 2 Tbsp.
4	2 cups	4 cups	1⅓ cups	1⅓ cups	1 tsp.	½ cup
5	2½ cups	5 cups	1⅔ cups	1⅔ cups	1¼ tsp.	½ cup + 2 Tbsp.
6	3 cups	6 cups	2 cups	2 cups	1½ tsp.	¾ cup

Instructions: Cook the oats and water according to oats package instructions. Mix in the other ingredients and heat, stirring, until everything is uniformly warm. Spoon into bowls and serve.

CREAMY STRAWBERRY SPICE

Ingredients: / No. of Servings:	oats	milk	straw-berries, sliced or mashed	cinna-mon	vanilla	yogurt (vanilla or straw-berry flavor)	brown sugar
1	½ cup	1 cup	½ cup	½ tsp.	½ tsp.	¼ cup	1½ Tbsp.
2	1 cup	2 cups	1 cup	1 tsp.	1 tsp.	½ cup	3 Tbsp.
3	1½ cups	3 cups	1½ cups	1½ tsp.	1½ tsp.	¾ cup	4½ Tbsp.
4	2 cups	4 cups	2 cups	2 tsp.	2 tsp.	1 cup	¼ cup + 2 Tbsp.
5	2½ cups	5 cups	2½ cups	2½ tsp.	2½ tsp.	1¼ cups	¼ cup + 3½ Tbsp.
6	3 cups	6 cups	3 cups	1 Tbsp.	1 Tbsp.	1½ cups	½ cup + 1 Tbsp.

Instructions: Cook the oats and milk according to oats package instructions. Mix in the other ingredients and heat, stirring, until everything is uniformly warm. (for a vegan option, use your favorite plant-based milk and yogurt) Spoon into bowls and serve.

PEGASUS' STRAWBERRY APPLE

Ingredients: No. of Servings:	oats	water	apple, diced	straw-berries	walnuts, chopped	brown sugar
1	½ cup	¾ cup	1 cup	½ cup	¼ cup	2 Tbsp.
2	1 cup	1½ cups	2 cups	1 cup	½ cup	¼ cup
3	1½ cups	2¼ cups	3 cups	1½ cups	¾ cup	¼ cup + 2 Tbsp.
4	2 cups	3 cups	4 cups	2 cups	1 cup	½ cup
5	2½ cups	3¾ cups	5 cups	2½ cups	1¼ cups	½ cup + 2 Tbsp.
6	3 cups	4¼ cups	6 cups	3 cups	1½ cups	¾ cup

Instructions: Puree the apple and strawberries in a blender with the water. Combine with oats and cook according to oats package instructions. Mix in the other ingredients and heat, stirring, until everything is uniformly warm. Spoon into bowls and serve.

SNOW WHITE AND ROSE RED'S WHITE CHOCOLATE STRAWBERRY

Ingredients: / No. of Servings:	oats	milk	vanilla	white chocolate chips	straw-berries, pureed	straw-berries, sliced
1	½ cup	1 cup	2 tsp.	¼ cup	½ cup	¼ cup
2	1 cup	2 cups	1 Tbsp. + 1 tsp.	½ cup	1 cup	½ cup
3	1½ cups	3 cups	2 Tbsp.	¾ cup	1½ cups	¾ cup
4	2 cups	4 cups	2 Tbsp. + 2 tsp.	1 cup	2 cups	1 cup
5	2½ cups	5 cups	3 Tbsp. + 1 tsp.	1¼ cups	2½ cups	1¼ cups
6	3 cups	6 cups	4 Tbsp.	1½ cups	3 cups	1½ cups

Instructions: Puree the first amount of strawberries in a blender with the milk. (For a vegan option, use your favorite plant-based milk.) Combine with the oats and cook according to oats package instructions. Mix in the vanilla and white chocolate chips. Heat, stirring, until white chocolate has melted and everything is uniformly warm. Spoon into bowls and add ¼ cup of sliced strawberries to the top of each portion before serving.

PEANUT BUTTER CHOCOLATE CHIP

Ingredients: No. of Servings:	oats	water	peanut butter	brown sugar	chocolate chips
1	½ cup	1 cup	3 Tbsp.	1 tsp.	¼ cup
2	1 cup	2 cups	¼ cup + 2 Tbsp.	2 tsp.	½ cup
3	1½ cups	3 cups	½ cup + 1 Tbsp.	1 Tbsp.	¾ cup
4	2 cups	4 cups	¾ cup	1 Tbsp. + 1 tsp.	1 cup
5	2½ cups	5 cups	¾ cup + 3 Tbsp.	1 Tbsp. + 2 tsp.	1¼ cups
6	3 cups	6 cups	1 cup + 2 Tbsp.	2 Tbsp.	1½ cups

Instructions: Cook the oats and water according to oats package instructions. Mix in the peanut butter and brown sugar and heat, stirring, until everything is uniformly warm. Spoon into bowls and sprinkle chocolate chips over each portion just before serving.

PEANUT BUTTER
CHOCOLATE CHIP
OATMEAL

THE PRINCESS AND THE PEANUT BUTTER

Ingredients: / No. of Servings:	oats	water	peanut butter	brown sugar
1	½ cup	1 cup	¼ cup	2 Tbsp.
2	1 cup	2 cups	½ cup	¼ cup
3	1½ cups	3 cups	¾ cup	¼ cup + 2 Tbsp.
4	2 cups	4 cups	1 cup	½ cup
5	2½ cups	5 cups	1¼ cups	½ cup + 2 Tbsp.
6	3 cups	6 cups	1½ cups	¾ cup

Instructions: Cook the oats and water according to oats package instructions. Mix in the other ingredients and heat, stirring, until everything is uniformly warm. Spoon into bowls and serve. If desired, sprinkle chopped peanuts over each serving.

BERRY PEANUT BUTTER

Ingredients: No. of Servings:	oats	water	berries	peanut butter	brown sugar
1	½ cup	1 cup	½ cup	3 Tbsp.	2 Tbsp.
2	1 cup	2 cups	1 cup	¼ cup + 2 Tbsp.	¼ cup
3	1½ cups	3 cups	1½ cups	½ cup + 1 Tbsp.	¼ cup + 2 Tbsp.
4	2 cups	4 cups	2 cups	¾ cup	½ cup
5	2½ cups	5 cups	2½ cups	¾ cup + 3 Tbsp.	½ cup + 2 Tbsp.
6	3 cups	6 cups	3 cups	1 cup + 2 Tbsp.	¾ cup

Instructions: Cook the oats and water according to oats package instructions. Mix in the other ingredients and heat until everything is uniformly warm. (You can use any kind of berries you like, but if you choose strawberries, I recommend chopping or pureeing them first.) Spoon into bowls and serve.

PEANUT BUTTER AND JELLY

Ingredients: No. of Servings:	oats	water	peanut butter	your favorite jam or jelly
1	½ cup	1 cup	3 Tbsp.	3 Tbsp.
2	1 cup	2 cups	¼ cup + 2 Tbsp.	¼ cup + 2 Tbsp.
3	1½ cups	3 cups	½ cup + 1 Tbsp.	½ cup + 1 Tbsp.
4	2 cups	4 cups	¾ cup	¾ cup
5	2½ cups	5 cups	¾ cup + 3 Tbsp.	¾ cup + 3 Tbsp.
6	3 cups	6 cups	1 cup + 2 Tbsp.	1 cup + 2 Tbsp.

Instructions: Cook the oats and water according to oats package instructions. Mix in the other ingredients and heat, stirring, until everything is uniformly warm. Spoon into bowls and serve.

PEANUT BUTTER & JELLY
OATMEAL

PEANUT BUTTER TRAIL MIX

Ingredients: / No. of Servings:	oats	water	your favorite trail mix	peanut butter	brown sugar
1	½ cup	1¼ cup	½ cup	2 Tbsp.	1 Tbsp.
2	1 cup	2½ cups	1 cup	¼ cup	2 Tbsp.
3	1½ cups	3¾ cups	1½ cups	¼ cup + 2 Tbsp.	3 Tbsp.
4	2 cups	5 cups	2 cups	½ cup	¼ cup
5	2½ cups	6¼ cups	2½ cups	½ cup + 2 Tbsp.	¼ cup + 1 Tbsp.
6	3 cups	7½ cups	3 cups	¾ cup	¼ cup + 2 Tbsp.

Instructions: Cook the oats and water according to oats package instructions. Mix in the other ingredients (adjust the amount of sugar depending on how sweet your trail mix is). Heat, stirring, until everything is uniformly warm. Spoon into bowls and serve.

APPLES AND PEANUT BUTTER

Ingredients: No. of Servings:	oats	water	apple, diced	peanut butter	brown sugar
1	½ cup	1 cup	¾ cup	2 Tbsp.	2 Tbsp.
2	1 cup	2 cups	1½ cups	¼ cup	¼ cup
3	1½ cups	3 cups	2¼ cups	¼ cup + 2 Tbsp.	¼ cup + 2 Tbsp.
4	2 cups	4 cups	3 cups	½ cup	½ cup
5	2½ cups	5 cups	3¾ cups	½ cup + 2 Tbsp.	½ cup + 2 Tbsp.
6	3 cups	6 cups	4½ cups	¾ cup	¾ cup

Instructions: Cook the oats and water according to oats package instructions. Mix in the other ingredients and heat, stirring, until everything is uniformly warm. Spoon into bowls and serve.

SNOW WHITE'S APPLE WALNUT

Ingredients: No. of Servings:	oats	water	apple, grated or finely chopped	walnuts, chopped	cinna- mon	salt	brown sugar
1	½ cup	1 cup	¾ cup	¼ cup	½ tsp.	⅛ tsp.	2 Tbsp.
2	1 cup	2 cups	1½ cups	½ cup	1 tsp.	¼ tsp.	¼ cup
3	1½ cups	3 cups	2¼ cups	¾ cup	1½ tsp.	⅜ tsp.	¼ cup + 2 Tbsp.
4	2 cups	4 cups	3 cups	1 cup	2 tsp.	½ tsp.	½ cup
5	2½ cups	5 cups	3¾ cups	1¼ cups	2½ tsp.	⅝ tsp.	½ cup + 2 Tbsp.
6	3 cups	6 cups	4½ cups	1½ cups	1 Tbsp.	¾ tsp.	¾ cup

Instructions: Cook the oats with the water and apple according to oats package instructions. Mix in the other ingredients and heat, stirring, until everything is uniformly warm. Spoon into bowls and serve.

MAPLE APPLE WITH PECANS

Ingredients: No. of Servings:	oats	water	pecans, chopped	apple, diced	maple syrup
1	½ cup	1 cup	¼ cup	¾ cup	2 Tbsp.
2	1 cup	2 cups	½ cup	1½ cups	¼ cup
3	1½ cups	3 cups	¾ cup	2¼ cups	¼ cup + 2 Tbsp.
4	2 cups	4 cups	1 cup	3 cups	½ cup
5	2½ cups	5 cups	1¼ cups	3¾ cups	½ cup + 2 Tbsp.
6	3 cups	6 cups	1½ cups	4½ cups	¾ cup

Instructions: Cook the oats and water according to oats package instructions. Mix in the other ingredients and heat, stirring, until everything is uniformly warm. Spoon into bowls and serve.

KING MIDAS' GOLDEN APPLESAUCE

Ingredients: / No. of Servings:	oats	water	applesauce	brown sugar
1	½ cup	⅔ cup	⅓ cup	2 Tbsp.
2	1 cup	1⅓ cups	⅔ cup	¼ cup
3	1½ cups	2 cups	1 cup	¼ cup + 2 Tbsp.
4	2 cups	2⅔ cups	1⅓ cups	½ cup
5	2½ cups	3⅓ cups	1⅔ cups	½ cup + 2 Tbsp.
6	3 cups	4 cups	2 cups	¾ cup

Instructions: Cook the oats with the water according to oats package instructions. Mix in the other ingredients. (I recommend using unsweetened applesauce. If yours is sweetened, you may want to decrease the sugar.) Heat, stirring, until everything is uniformly warm. Spoon into bowls and serve.

DRAGON'S HOARD: GOLDEN APPLESAUCE RAISIN

Ingredients: No. of Servings:	oats	water	apple-sauce	raisins	walnuts, chopped	cinna-mon	brown sugar
1	½ cup	¾ cup	⅓ cup	¼ cup	3 Tbsp.	¼ tsp.	2 Tbsp.
2	1 cup	1½ cups	⅔ cup	½ cup	¼ cup + 2 Tbsp.	½ tsp.	¼ cup
3	1½ cups	2¼ cups	1 cup	¾ cup	½ cup + 1 Tbsp.	¾ tsp.	¼ cup + 2 Tbsp.
4	2 cups	3 cups	1⅓ cups	1 cup	¾ cup	1 tsp.	½ cup
5	2½ cups	3¾ cups	1⅔ cups	1¼ cups	¾ cup + 3 Tbsp.	1 ¼ tsp.	½ cup + 2 Tbsp.
6	3 cups	4½ cups	2 cups	1½ cups	1 cup + 2 Tbsp.	1 ½ tsp.	¾ cup

Instructions: Cook the oats and water according to oats package instructions. Mix in the other ingredients and heat, stirring, until everything is uniformly warm. (I recommend using unsweetened applesauce. If yours is sweetened, you may want to decrease the sugar.) Spoon into bowls and serve.

RUMPELSTILTSKIN'S RAISIN CREAM CHEESE

Ingredients: / No. of Servings:	oats	milk	cream cheese	raisins and/or other dried fruit	vanilla	cinna-mon	brown sugar
1	½ cup	1 cup	2 Tbsp.	⅓ cup	¼ tsp.	½ tsp.	2 Tbsp.
2	1 cup	2 cups	¼ cup	⅔ cup	½ tsp.	1 tsp.	¼ cup
3	1½ cups	3 cups	¼ cup + 2 Tbsp.	1 cup	¾ tsp.	1½ tsp.	¼ cup + 2 Tbsp.
4	2 cups	4 cups	½ cup	1⅓ cups	1 tsp.	2 tsp.	½ cup
5	2½ cups	5 cups	½ cup + 2 Tbsp.	1⅔ cups	1¼ tsp.	2½ tsp.	½ cup + 2 Tbsp.
6	3 cups	6 cups	¾ cup	2 cups	1½ tsp.	1 Tbsp.	¾ cup

Instructions: Cook the oats and milk according to oats package instructions. Mix in the other ingredients. (For a vegan option, use your favorite plant-based milk and cream cheese.) Try experimenting with different combinations of dried fruit. If they're sweetened, you may want to reduce or skip the brown sugar. Heat, stirring, until everything is uniformly warm. Spoon into bowls and serve.

BLUEBEARD'S BLUEBERRY CREAM CHEESE

Ingredients: / No. of Servings:	oats	milk	cream cheese	blue-berries	maple syrup
1	½ cup	1 cup	¼ cup	½ cup	2 Tbsp.
2	1 cup	2 cups	½ cup	1 cup	¼ cup
3	1½ cups	3 cups	¾ cup	1½ cups	¼ cup + 2 Tbsp.
4	2 cups	4 cups	1 cup	2 cups	½ cup
5	2½ cups	5 cups	1¼ cups	2½ cups	½ cup + 2 Tbsp.
6	3 cups	6 cups	1½ cups	3 cups	¾ cup

Instructions: Cook the oats and milk according to oats package instructions. Mix in the other ingredients (for a vegan option, use your favorite plant-based milk and cream cheese) and heat, stirring, until everything is uniformly warm. Spoon into bowls and serve.

BLUEBERRY WHITE CHOCOLATE

Ingredients: / No. of Servings:	oats	water	blue-berries	white chocolate chips
1	½ cup	1 cup	¾ cup	⅓ cup
2	1 cup	2 cups	1½ cups	⅔ cup
3	1½ cups	3 cups	2¼ cups	1 cup
4	2 cups	4 cups	3 cups	1⅓ cups
5	2½ cups	5 cups	3¾ cups	1⅔ cups
6	3 cups	6 cups	4½ cups	2 cups

Instructions: Cook the oats and water according to oats package instructions. Mix in the other ingredients and heat, stirring, until white chocolate has melted and everything is uniformly warm. Spoon into bowls and serve. If desired, sprinkle additional white chocolate chips over each serving.

BLUEBERRY
WHITE CHOCOLATE
OATMEAL

LITTLE BOY BLUEBERRY PECAN

Ingredients: No. of Servings:	oats	water	blue-berries	pecans, toasted and chopped	brown sugar
1	½ cup	1 cup	¾ cup	⅓ cup	2 Tbsp.
2	1 cup	2 cups	1 ½ cups	⅔ cup	¼ cup
3	1 ½ cups	3 cups	2 ¼ cups	1 cup	¼ cup + 2 Tbsp.
4	2 cups	4 cups	3 cups	1 ⅓ cups	½ cup
5	2 ½ cups	5 cups	3 ¾ cups	1 ⅔ cups	½ cup + 2 Tbsp.
6	3 cups	6 cups	4½ cups	2 cups	¾ cup

Instructions: Cook the oats and water according to oats package instructions. Mix in the other ingredients and heat, stirring, until everything is uniformly warm. Spoon into bowls and serve.

WIZARD'S PURPLE POTION: CREAMY BLUEBERRY

Ingredients: No. of Servings:	oats	water	milk	coconut milk	blue-berries	lemon juice and vanilla	brown sugar
1	½ cup	¼ cup	½ cup	¼ cup	½ cup	½ tsp. each	2 Tbsp.
2	1 cup	½ cup	1 cup	½ cup	1 cup	1 tsp. each	¼ cup
3	1½ cups	¾ cup	1½ cups	¾ cup	1½ cups	1½ tsp. each	¼ cup + 2 Tbsp.
4	2 cups	1 cup	2 cups	1 cup	2 cups	2 tsp. each	½ cup
5	2½ cups	1¼ cups	2½ cups	1¼ cups	2½ cups	2½ tsp. each	½ cup + 2 Tbsp.
6	3 cups	1½ cups	3 cups	1½ cups	3 cups	1 Tbsp. each	¾ cup

Instructions: Puree the blueberries in a blender with the water. Combine with the milk and coconut milk (for a vegan option, omit the milk and triple the coconut milk) and oats and cook according to oats package instructions. Mix in the other ingredients and heat, stirring, until everything is uniformly warm. Spoon into bowls and serve.

BLUEBERRY COCONUT

Ingredients: / No. of Servings:	oats	water	coconut milk	blue-berries	grated coconut	brown sugar
1	½ cup	½ cup	½ cup	½ cup	2 Tbsp.	2 Tbsp.
2	1 cup	1 cup	1 cup	1 cup	¼ cup	¼ cup
3	1½ cups	1½ cups	1½ cups	1½ cups	¼ cup + 2 Tbsp.	¼ cup + 2 Tbsp.
4	2 cups	2 cups	2 cups	2 cups	½ cup	½ cup
5	2½ cups	2½ cups	2½ cups	2½ cups	½ cup + 2 Tbsp.	½ cup + 2 Tbsp.
6	3 cups	3 cups	3 cups	3 cups	¾ cup	¾ cup

Instructions: Cook the oats, water, and coconut milk according to oats package instructions. Mix in the other ingredients and heat, stirring, until everything is uniformly warm. Spoon into bowls and serve.

BLUEBERRY COCONUT CASHEW

Ingredients: No. of Servings:	oats	water	blue-berries	cashews, toasted and chopped	grated coconut	vanilla	brown sugar
1	½ cup	1 cup	½ cup	⅓ cup	2 Tbsp.	½ tsp.	2 Tbsp.
2	1 cup	2 cups	1 cup	⅔ cup	¼ cup	1 tsp.	¼ cup
3	1 ½ cups	3 cups	1 ½ cups	1 cup	¼ cup + 2 Tbsp.	1 ½ tsp.	¼ cup + 2 Tbsp.
4	2 cups	4 cups	2 cups	1 ⅓ cups	½ cup	2 tsp.	½ cup
5	2 ½ cups	5 cups	2 ½ cups	1 ⅔ cups	½ cup + 2 Tbsp.	2 ½ tsp.	½ cup + 2 Tbsp.
6	3 cups	6 cups	3 cups	2 cups	¾ cup	1 Tbsp.	¾ cup

Instructions: Cook the oats and water according to oats package instructions. Mix in the other ingredients and heat, stirring, until everything is uniformly warm. Spoon into bowls and serve.

PINEAPPLE CASHEW

Ingredients: / No. of Servings:	oats	water	coconut milk	pineapple, chopped	cashews, toasted and chopped	brown sugar
1	½ cup	⅔ cups	⅓ cup	½ cup	2 Tbsp.	2 Tbsp.
2	1 cup	1 ⅓ cups	⅔ cup	1 cup	¼ cup	¼ cup
3	1 ½ cups	2 cups	1 cup	1 ½ cups	¼ cup + 2 Tbsp.	¼ cup + 2 Tbsp.
4	2 cups	2 ⅔ cups	1 ⅓ cups	2 cups	½ cup	½ cup
5	2 ½ cups	3 ⅓ cups	1 ⅔ cups	2 ½ cups	½ cup + 2 Tbsp.	½ cup + 2 Tbsp.
6	3 cups	4 cups	2 cups	3 cups	¾ cup	¾ cup

Instructions: Cook the oats, water, and coconut milk according to oats package instructions. Mix in the other ingredients and heat, stirring, until everything is uniformly warm. Spoon into bowls and serve.

BANANA NUT

Ingredients: / No. of Servings:	oats	water	bananas, mashed	your favorite nuts, chopped	cinnamon	brown sugar
1	½ cup	1 cup	1	¼ cup	¼ tsp.	2 Tbsp.
2	1 cup	2 cups	2	½ cup	½ tsp.	¼ cup
3	1½ cups	3 cups	3	¾ cup	¾ tsp.	¼ cup + 2 Tbsp.
4	2 cups	4 cups	4	1 cup	1 tsp.	½ cup
5	2½ cups	5 cups	5	1¼ cups	1¼ tsp.	½ cup + 2 Tbsp.
6	3 cups	6 cups	6	1½ cups	1½ tsp.	¾ cup

Instructions: Cook the oats and water according to oats package instructions. Mix in the other ingredients and heat, stirring, until everything is uniformly warm. Spoon into bowls and serve.

BANANA SPICE

Ingredients: No. of Servings:	oats	water	bananas, mashed	walnuts, chopped	cinna-mon	ginger	nutmeg	vanil-la	brown sugar
1	½ cup	1 cup	1	3 Tbsp.	¼ tsp.	⅛ tsp.	1 dash	½ tsp.	2 Tbsp.
2	1 cup	2 cups	2	¼ cup + 2 Tbsp.	½ tsp.	¼ tsp.	2 dashes	1 tsp.	¼ cup
3	1½ cups	3 cups	3	½ cup + 1 Tbsp.	¾ tsp.	⅜ tsp.	3 dashes	1½ tsp.	¼ cup + 2 Tbsp.
4	2 cups	4 cups	4	¾ cup	1 tsp.	½ tsp.	4 dashes	2 tsp.	½ cup
5	2½ cups	5 cups	5	¾ cup + 3 Tbsp.	1¼ tsp.	⅝ tsp.	5 dashes	2½ tsp.	½ cup + 2 Tbsp.
6	3 cups	6 cups	6	1 cup + 2 Tbsp.	1½ tsp.	¾ tsp.	6 dashes	1 Tbsp.	¾ cup

Instructions: Cook the oats and water according to oats package instructions. Mix in the other ingredients and heat, stirring, until everything is uniformly warm. Spoon into bowls and serve.

BANANA SPICE OATMEAL

BANANA ORANGE SPICE

Ingredients: No. of Servings:	oats	water	orange juice	bananas, mashed	cinna-mon	ground cloves	brown sugar
1	½ cup	½ cup	½ cup	1	¼ tsp.	⅛ tsp.	2 Tbsp.
2	1 cup	1 cup	1 cup	2	½ tsp.	¼ tsp.	¼ cup
3	1 ½ cups	1 ½ cups	1 ½ cups	3	¾ tsp.	⅜ tsp.	¼ cup + 2 Tbsp.
4	2 cups	2 cups	2 cups	4	1 tsp.	½ tsp.	½ cup
5	2 ½ cups	2 ½ cups	2 ½ cups	5	1 ¼ tsp.	⅝ tsp.	½ cup + 2 Tbsp.
6	3 cups	3 cups	3 cups	6	1 ½ tsp.	¾ tsp.	¾ cup

Instructions: Cook the oats, water, and orange juice according to oats package instructions. Mix in the other ingredients and heat, stirring, until everything is uniformly warm. Spoon into bowls and serve.

CHOCOLATE BANANA

Ingredients: / No. of Servings:	oats	water	bananas, mashed	vanilla	chocolate syrup
1	½ cup	1 cup	1	½ tsp.	2 Tbsp.
2	1 cup	2 cups	2	1 tsp.	¼ cup
3	1½ cups	3 cups	3	1½ tsp.	¼ cup + 2 Tbsp.
4	2 cups	4 cups	4	2 tsp.	½ cup
5	2½ cups	5 cups	5	2½ tsp.	½ cup + 2 Tbsp.
6	3 cups	6 cups	6	1 Tbsp.	¾ cup

Instructions: Cook the oats and water according to oats package instructions. Mix in the other ingredients and heat, stirring, until everything is uniformly warm. Spoon into bowls and serve.

BANANA PEANUT BUTTER

Ingredients: No. of Servings:	oats	water	small bananas, mashed	peanut butter	honey	cinnamon
1	½ cup	1 cup	1	3 Tbsp.	2 Tbsp.	¼ tsp.
2	1 cup	2 cups	2	¼ cup + 2 Tbsp.	¼ cup	½ tsp.
3	1½ cups	3 cups	3	½ cup + 1 Tbsp.	¼ cup + 2 Tbsp.	¾ tsp.
4	2 cups	4 cups	4	¾ cup	½ cup	1 tsp.
5	2½ cups	5 cups	5	¾ cup + 3 Tbsp.	½ cup + 2 Tbsp.	1¼ tsp.
6	3 cups	6 cups	6	1 cup + 2 Tbsp.	¾ cup	1½ tsp.

Instructions: Cook the oats and water according to oats package instructions. Mix in the other ingredients (for a vegan option, use Bee Free Honee or another honey substitute) and heat, stirring, until everything is uniformly warm. Spoon into bowls and serve.

BANANA PEANUT BUTTER
OATMEAL

TRUE LOVE'S KISS: CARAMEL BANANA WITH PEANUT BUTTER

Ingredients: No. of Servings:	oats	water	bananas, mashed	caramel syrup	peanut butter
1	½ cup	1 cup	1	2 Tbsp.	3 Tbsp.
2	1 cup	2 cups	2	¼ cup	¼ cup + 2 Tbsp.
3	1½ cups	3 cups	3	¼ cup + 2 Tbsp.	½ cup + 1 Tbsp.
4	2 cups	4 cups	4	½ cup	¾ cup
5	2½ cups	5 cups	5	½ cup + 2 Tbsp.	¾ cup + 3 Tbsp.
6	3 cups	6 cups	6	¾ cup	1 cup + 2 Tbsp.

Instructions: Cook the oats and water according to oats package instructions. Mix in the other ingredients and heat, stirring, until everything is uniformly warm. Spoon into bowls and serve.

TROLL UNDER THE BRIDGE'S NUTTY CRUNCH

Ingredients: No. of Servings:	oats	water	peanuts, cashews, almonds, and pecans (all toasted and finely chopped)	walnuts, chopped	bananas, mashed	maple syrup
1	½ cup	1 cup	1 Tbsp. of each	2 Tbsp.	½	2 Tbsp.
2	1 cup	2 cups	2 Tbsp. of each	¼ cup	1	¼ cup
3	1½ cups	3 cups	3 Tbsp. of each	¼ cup + 2 Tbsp.	1½	¼ cup + 2 Tbsp.
4	2 cups	4 cups	¼ cup of each	½ cup	2	½ cup
5	2½ cups	5 cups	¼ cup + 1 Tbsp. of each	½ cup + 2 Tbsp.	2½	½ cup + 2 Tbsp.
6	3 cups	6 cups	¼ cup + 2 Tbsp. of each	¾ cup	3	¾ cup

Instructions: Cook the oats and water according to oats package instructions. Mix in the other ingredients and heat, stirring, until everything is uniformly warm. Spoon into bowls and serve.

BILLY GOAT GRUFF'S NUTTY CRUNCH II

Ingredients: No. of Servings:	oats	water	wheat germ, grated coconut, sunflower seeds, cashews, almonds, pumpkin seeds, pecans (all toasted and finely chopped)	walnuts, chopped	ground flax seed	brown sugar
1	⅓ cup	1 cup	1 Tbsp. each	2 Tbsp.	1 tsp.	2 Tbsp.
2	⅔ cup	2 cups	2 Tbsp. each	¼ cup	2 tsp.	¼ cup
3	1 cups	3 cups	3 Tbsp. each	¼ cup + 2 Tbsp.	1 Tbsp.	¼ cup + 2 Tbsp.
4	1⅓ cups	4 cups	¼ cup each	½ cup	1 Tbsp. + 1 tsp.	½ cup
5	1⅔ cups	5 cups	¼ cup + 1 Tbsp. each	½ cup + 2 Tbsp.	1 Tbsp. + 2 tsp.	½ cup + 2 Tbsp.
6	2 cups	6 cups	¼ cup + 2 Tbsp. each	¾ cup	2 Tbsp.	¾ cup

Instructions: Cook the oats with the water according to oats package instructions. Mix in the other ingredients (fill your spoon or cup measures heaping full of the nuts and seeds, not flat). Heat, stirring, until everything is uniformly warm. Spoon into bowls and serve.

PETER RABBIT'S CARROT CAKE

Ingredients: / No. of Servings:	oats	water	carrot, grated	cream cheese	walnuts, chopped	cinna-mon and vanilla	ginger	brown sugar	nutmeg
1	½ cup	1⅓ cups	⅓ cup	3 Tbsp.	¼ cup	½ tsp. each	⅛ tsp.	2 Tbsp.	1 sprinkle
2	1 cup	2⅔ cups	⅔ cup	¼ cup + 2 Tbsp.	½ cup	1 tsp. each	¼ tsp.	¼ cup	2 sprinkles
3	1½ cups	4 cups	1 cup	½ cup + 1 Tbsp.	¾ cup	1½ tsp. each	⅜ tsp.	¼ cup + 2 Tbsp.	3 sprinkles
4	2 cups	5⅓ cups	1⅓ cups	¾ cup	1 cup	2 tsp. each	½ tsp.	½ cup	4 sprinkles
5	2½ cups	6⅔ cups	1⅔ cups	¾ cup + 3 Tbsp.	1¼ cups	2½ tsp. each	⅝ tsp.	½ cup + 2 Tbsp.	5 sprinkles
6	3 cups	8 cups	2 cups	1 cup + 2 Tbsp.	1½ cups	1 Tbsp. each	¾ tsp.	¾ cup	6 sprinkles

Instructions: Combine the water and grated carrots and cook for a few minutes on the stovetop or in the microwave until carrots are soft. Add the oats and cook according to oats package instructions. Mix in the other ingredients, except for the nutmeg, and heat, stirring, until everything is uniformly warm. (For a vegan option, use your favorite plant-based cream cheese.) Spoon into bowls and sprinkle the nutmeg over each portion before serving.

I HOPE YOU ENJOYED THESE RECIPES!

If you did, would you please leave a review on Amazon? You can do it at http://smarturl.it/OnceUponOatmeal. Even one or two sentences would be a big help. Thank you!

ABOUT THE AUTHOR

Annie Douglass Lima considers herself fortunate to have traveled in twenty different countries and lived in four of them. A fifth-grade teacher in her "other" life, she loves reading to her students and sparking their imaginations. Her books include science fiction, fantasy, YA action and adventure novels, a puppet script, anthologies of her students' poetry, Bible verse coloring and activity books, and now a cookbook. When she isn't teaching, writing, or experimenting with new flavors of oatmeal, Annie can often be found sipping spiced chai or pomegranate green tea in exotic locations, some of which exist in this world.

Connect with Me Online

Facebook: http://www.facebook.com/AnnieDouglassLimaAuthor

Smashwords: https://www.smashwords.com/profile/view/AnnieDouglassLima

Goodreads: http://bit.ly/ADLimaOnGoodreads

Blog: http://anniedouglasslima.blogspot.com

Twitter: https://twitter.com/princeofalasia

Email: AnnieDouglassLima@gmail.com

Sign up for my mailing list so I can let you know when new books are available. When you sign up, I'll send you a free copy of one of my fantasy books! http://bit.ly/LimaUpdates

Printed in Great Britain
by Amazon